After Following

poems

After Following

poems

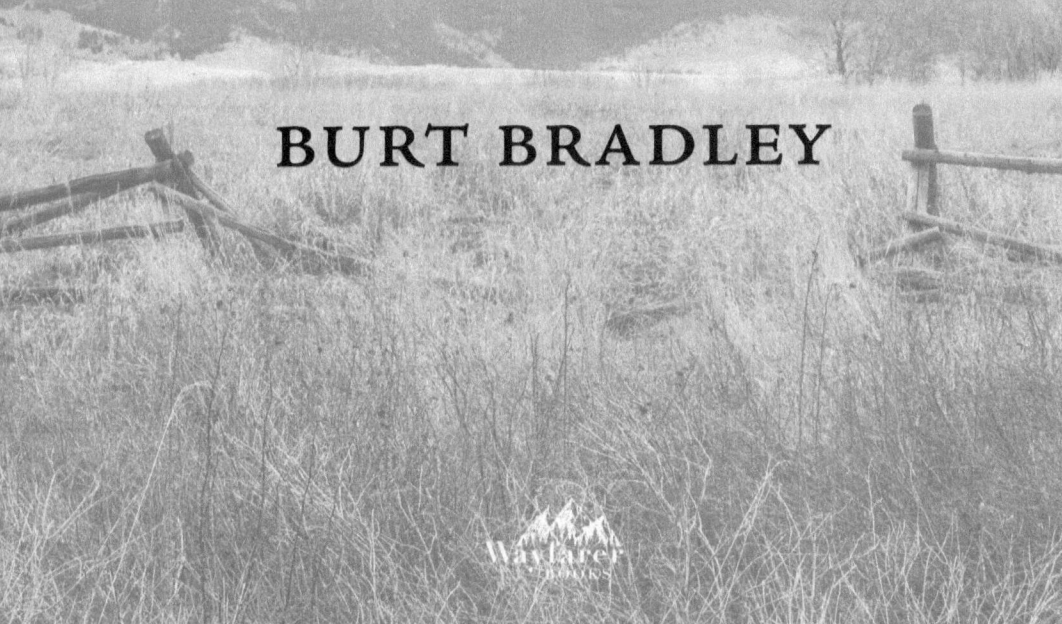

BURT BRADLEY

Wayfarer
BOOKS

WAYFARER BOOKS
WWW.WAYFARERBOOKS.ORG

Published in 2019 · Homebound Publications

Front Cover Image © Dane Deaner

Cover and Interior Designed by Leslie M. Browning

first edition · 9781947003422

second edition 978-1-965320-19-8

Published by Wayfarer Books 2024

10 9 8 7 6 5 4 3 2

Wayfarer Books is committed to ecological stewardship.
We greatly value the natural environment and invest in conservation.

PO Box 1601, Northampton, MA 01060

wayfarer@homeboundpublications.com

WAYFARERBOOKS.ORG

For Janet

Contents

An Open Prayer to W. B. Yeats

Unlike you, I have no tower
of symbols, no great lust for Helen of Troy,
no Maude Gonne to fall madly over
for years, and no Madam Blavatsky
(thank God and all seven orders of angels).

Just this rose, this skinny bush
climbing my porch, thorny green
with rouge, red flowers half
wilted now from the hundred
degree heat like blotches of dried blood.
They are more a symbol
of poor watering than anything mystical.

Still, I won't let them go or this poem
even as night descends
like an electric blanket on high,
smothering the moon, a sad crescent,
and these roses now drooping shadows,
the blossoms gratefully erased,
the thorns dulled by darkness.

But, this world, unlike Blake's
treed angels or your widening gyres,
clings to dot.coms caught still buzzing
in a world-wide web, sans spider,
patternless, and consumer ridden.

So, I pray for your help, my dear Yeats.
I'll take one fake fairy, or one occult fib,
even some mumbo-jumbo automatic writing—
new metaphors or dead—for any vision:
even with glasses, rose-colored or cracked
is better than no vision at all.

Page From the Diary of a Faithful Husband

(following Anne Sexton)

My last affair was a caravan
across endless dunes on humped beasts
jangling in the air heavy with jasmine.
I would shun the tent to bathe my eyes
in the deep iridescent pool of night.
She was never a *girl* to lie with me,
but older, unfathomable, tidal,
her hips like glazed jars of olive oil,
her belly Mediterranean round,
earth brown with a rubied naval.

I didn't care anymore if her breasts
were not pomegranates from Solomon's garden,
or were still aching from the gritty palms of her last lover,
a camel driver and petty thief who loved women
more than money, who loved to drink wine
from a goatskin bag, letting it bleed down his chin,
who would spend forty days in the desert
where he wrote poetry in the sand
and danced naked beneath every full moon.

I didn't care if she loved him for all that
and because he didn't ask anything of her
but to dip his tongue into her honey, to hear her laugh,
which is all I said I wanted, but she saw clear
through me and my muddy intentions,

knowing the storm I was, not just rain
out of context, but flood, deluge, and utterly arkless,
that I'd turn the desert into nothing
but an ocean floor again teeming
with crustaceans, coral, the bones
of old wrecks and sunken treasure.

Tonight, the rain is delicious.
During a shiny, wet dusk, silver coins spill
onto the glassed roof of the greenhouse.

It strikes me as the most sensual of sounds,
a moist rhythm, more desirable than the sea salt taste of sex.
I don't care anymore for lovers, just a little water
now and then dripping from the eaves.

Winter Sunrise When There
are Flamingos to Remember By

(following Dylan Thomas)

The earth rolls out of its darkness,
leaving last night's cutthroat wind behind,
crumpled and dissipated beneath the triumph
of emaciated trees. Winter slows
to shuffling, kindly, old, and balding,
down the street as the first light lifts
like a flock of neon flamingos,
luridly pink wherever there is sky.

I remember under the pillow sleight of hand
of rootless teeth into solid silver coins.
I remember, too, the green mischief of St. Patrick's Day
and Halloween's orange and black thrills.
I would remember more, but the flamingos go magenta
and a million wings flap into deafening reds,
fuchsias, and vermillion that just as soon disappear
leaving nothing to the imagination,
but this little yellow light.

Sagebrush Sutra

(after Allen Ginsburg)

During a drought, its favorite climate,
it smells bitter as an old dollar bill,
the kind soda machines won't take.
It is ubiquitously ugly, and the color
of the last place in the world.
It's why lizards mate, and antelope,
who are faster than cheetahs, never run.

It's the only lover of rattlesnakes
and living death to certain kinds of rain.
It's where chalky soil finds a home
and cactus a brother. It's the holy bush
without fire, the devil's pillow when he's tired.

It's the end of civilization and the beginning
of what we can't imagine.
It is where artists find their inspiration
and how they lose it.
It was the first thing to grow outside
the Garden, and the last thing to die
before the Apocalypse.

It is not heart, not mind, not Buddha
even when everything else is.
It's why cats make the same awful violin sound

when they fight or fuck,
and why dogs far away bark
at nothing on the quietest nights.

It has something to do with jet engines
and a little with unmarked cars.
It is the absolute proof of E=MC2,
the certitude in the uncertainty principle,
and concrete evidence of God's existence.
It took root in the last second before the Big Bang
and is the secret material found in Cupid's arrows
and Thor's hammer, and the last thing,
beneath hope, in Pandora's box.

It's a reedy, pungent bush,
that doesn't care a fig about us,
and yet if we ignore it, we miss
one of the gateless gates to heaven
on earth.

War Against Iraq

(following Berryman)

Where is Henry in this bloody war,
that ended without ending?
Long, long he fell ago
from a benign bridge with a view
of the bland streets of Minneapolis.
A model, *They* say, for Baghdad,
when we wipe out this "axis of evil" that lies
nearest to the petroleum dear to our hearts.

Henry, don't come back. Don't roll away
any stones. Don't even think resurrection,
though godknows we need a savior.
They'll be no breaking of our glasses
in the hearth. No hip, hip, hooray.
No for he's the jolly good fellow.
No world safe from democracy.

After a Spring Snow
(after Neruda)

To squeeze time like some fat orange
pulpy between my palms,
the rind grinding into rough peelings,
the juice, a taste of space itself,
neither syrup thick, a sky clotted with stars,
nor thin as grain alcohol gone
as it pools in a flame of dry air.

Spring isn't a time, but an invitation
to embrace the fruits of decay.
What's left to do, but drink in the citric moment,
so the fruitless boredom that hangs heavy
on the unconscious falls to rot where it may.
Only to gather again, anew, the bunches of snow,
and find the cold pavement ripening with prints,
paws, soles, and canes: first tastings of the earth.

Elegy for Craig Arnold

(for Rebecca)

Volcanoes are fuming hermits,
angry recluses who belch smoke
and spit fire, shunning any and all
who dare approach their grumbling huts.

                     Still, this poet
of the emotional underworld dared,
approaching like Odysseus, who drew
the shades to him, and from each gathered the knowledge
of the heart's inner desires and defeats. So,

                     he, too, was drawn
like a lover to the siren call of this adventure,
Was it the dark uncomfortable reserve
he *took upon himself,* willingly
taking the risk, not to endure the heat,
but the cooling, the hardening, even the dormancy?

                     It couldn't have been simple
curiosity or material for a book, but a pilgrimage,
a paying homage, this searcher for the sacred,
and in blessing was blessed, this deliberate wanderer
to an inarticulate place which had spent its rage,
become mute, artless, anonymous

                    until he arrived
bringing vocabulary as he ascended to the edge
of this ancient birth canal, called volcano,
born from Vulcan, hammering fire,
and vulva, fiery nativity, birthed and ruptured
into rapture—lyrics born of the underworld
ghosts of the flaming earth swirling up.

                    He listened,
leaning toward their dark sensual, once hot voices
spewing pure poetry into his waxless ear,
and unbound by pedestrian punctuation—no periods
to stop him, no pauses either were pulled—

                    -yanked!
(no doubt, he thought, a good word choice)
by the dark god himself who heard the tumultuous passion
of spring, again in the poet's words and taken, half
laughing, to completion, to be written on the fumes
and embedded in the molten soil to ash, yes,
to the final fluttering of ash:

                    to be
dispersed, carried on the winds, by invisible birds
and dropped into shells, into seeds—pomegranates no less—
filling all the pauses, the deferments, the caesuras,
the silent bridges between loss and gain,
lust and love, words and flesh,
                    poetry and earth.

Lament for Lorca

I can see him even from this far away,
manacled, his oiled hair hanging,
the poor teacher chained to him
like starved circus elephants side by side
toward their huge gray fate,
marched out of the jail into the night,
July, swollen with heat and panting,
too sick to open its lunar eyes.

I see them at the top of the hill,
Granada sleeping fitfully below.
Disappearing over the rise, the soldiers,
young enough to still love death,
their uniforms, unstained by war,
crackle in the darkness, the aching leather
holsters and boots scuffing the earth.

His voice slices through them, a shark,
blueblack sheen, like unglazed mercury,
a song sung under the waves sharpened
by a green moon blades their dark heads,
cleaving their deaf and mute hearts:

"Porque quiero dormir el sueño
de las manzanas para aprender
un llanto que me limpie de tierra."
"For I want to sleep the dream
of the apples, to learn a lament
that will cleanse me of the earth."

late spring night storm

(following e.e. cummings)

@ half past one a.m. may almost
full, while all the flowering
smells are squeezed inside a grave
darkness, the stars one
by one wiped out,
the moon m.i.a.
as this distraught wind
weeps for everything (&
nothing in particular): no one
drowns for long as the world sinks
into what it was *a priori*
this *coitus interruptus*.

Following Kahlil Gibran in Winter

You must walk out past the lights
where winter lies untouched
at the end of February, the fields half
nothing, half melted,
wearing colorless robes of earth.

You must wait until night
when the little sun, lost
most of the day, finally loses
itself in the naked darkness.

You must stand out there,
late, starless, with a moon
shunned by the clouds
hanging over your head.

When a twinge of cold wind
will awaken you to this life
that is half your own.

The rest lies in this iron silence
that rings with the mystery of
your hope, and the wonder
in your wonder at the world.

The Death of Autumn
(after Picasso)

There's no falling,
nothing left to fall,
not skin and bones,
but skinned, deboned,
the disembodied body
of the earth being made
into spirit, ghost of whiteness,
but for the thickening torsos
of people, growing wool,
flannel, walking coat trees,
knitted heads, muffled ears,
fleeced-line fingers,
in bear feet.

50th Birthday Beneath a Harvest Moon

(following W.S. Merwin)

Sometimes I think it isn't all about light.
Candles on a birthday cake,
the puffed cheeks, the breath
blown like an untied balloon,
everybody applauding: half a century.

The moon nothing, an orbiting rock,
temperatureless, unlit itself,
circling as if nothing else matters,
not the stolen light anyway,
(something we have in common),
but the circling, the invisible pull,
the tidal blood, the hunter's advantage,
the lunacy known by all bartenders,
emergency rooms, and Viking wives.

Too much light even for the blind,
though somebody will notice.
Galapagos tortoise—two hundred years old,
California Giant Sequoia—five, six centuries,
and this great heaving globe—a mere four billion.
No cake for any of it. No cessation.

The sea ebbs, the tortoise pulls away
from the shore where the sea wrack washes up

on the coast flooding the inlands
with salt, bleaching the roots,
urging everything toward the night sky,
toward that bright hole in the darkness.

Toward that old mirror of light
into which our planet looks
admiring her face, its ability to thicken
and thin, and whether full or empty,
able to move the ageless seas,
where whales sing great blue birthday songs.

The Flood, A Wyoming Love Song
(after T.S. Eliot)

It rained all these days in a row,
not a little and not a lot. Never was
it known for what it was in the day,
always half dismal and too long.

Only at night, sunk deep
into the inchoate darkness
when the drowning began:
the death of dryness, of the brittle,
of the crisp, the definite, and the earth
lost ground. We began to understand

the amphibian, later the gill and the fin,
until we knew the earliest we had been:
that first swirling and first tide,
that first brooding and breath,
the seamless seam between great and small,

and nothing between what was thinking
and what was thought, what was thought
and what was. And after that,
not a drop for so long that the rain
became a fiction, dried to a myth,
evaporated faithfully into a belief
in things unseen.

West of Duffy's Farm

(after James Wright)

It's not a hammock.
But one of those old aluminum chairs,
painted green once, I think,
now, the color of all the seasons together.

It's not unfamiliar,
but the kind my grandparents sat in,
on their patio for half a century,
turbulent years that ended in rust and cancer.
Still, the chairs sat well, solid,
decaying gracefully.

It's not Minnesota either.
But, Wyoming, by God, chiseled, gouged and split,
with bones protruding since the last ice age.
The work goes on, the wind last night
hammering clouds and trees to smithereens.

And it's not Duffy's farm.
But a studio, Giarrizzo's—a farmer of color,
with fields of paint sown in his blood
and brush, harvesting shapes of light.

Waiting for his return,
the sun flecking our dogs,
his, the color of red ale,

mine, a murder of crows on snow,
I sit in a self-portrait of why
I haven't wasted all of my life.

Belated Letter to James Wright

Dear Jim,

     Can you believe it, Jim, we meet at last? You through at fifty-two, me beginning, yes again, I know! But between Ohio and Wyoming lies Sacramento, my Martin's Ferry. I'll trade your glass factory for a discount welfare grocery store. I thought I'd never get out and did, stumbling for a while, numb to my own passion for poetry. I fell in with Wordsworth, dreamy and wonderful, with Whitman—excitable, goofy, out of blessed control. I followed them not knowing any better, anything. I was alone, too. But it would take decades before I got to Roethke and Hugo except that I could drink and did, stumbling—an art now—through a glass after glass darkly. Like I said, numbed and ignorant of iambic anything, I rambled, blurred, bleary-eyed and hoarse, an ear only for sentiment, not real sounds, though one can't do without the other, like lichen, like juniper and pinyon pine. Despite my passion, I had no skill, no training, like some schizophrenic attempting to play a violin for the first time, frenetically sawing the bow across the strings, the sounds were fast and loud but painfully unmusical, not even to scale. Here I am. A thief, a pirate, a pretender to an invisible throne, come to your vault—a hammock for Christ's sake—into which I dive, head first, ass up like some Looney Tunes character, spinning the contraption into a cocoon. But in there, between the trees, I will sing, the material muffling my song about blessing the fibers, the threads, the weave, the loom, and the field of light where you worked without wasting a particle or wave.

                                   Bless you,

                                   B.

A Very Old Man Smoking his Last Cigar

(following Wallace Stevens)

The sun, a heavy apple, Golden
Delicious, ripens as it falls
from a blue limb of sky.

The taste of bark on his tongue,
autumn smoke, old browned leaves
withering the air, he breathes
in the last of the light

and knows the transparent weave of life
and death and life, his being
a singular thread wound from an invisible ball
before his birth: at times, taut
as a harp string, other hours looped

softly in a coil of breeze
tangling a moment, knotted
to where there seems no more to be lengthened

and then, rain, like a magician's hands,
lubricating, kneading his existence out
again, in a line, absolutely level as a beam

of silver moonlight, iridescent,
illuminating itself and a way
through the labyrinth of minotaurs and virgins

past the myth of darkness to the flower
blooming in the blueblack curve of space beyond
his imagination: where he thought
it was all to end.

Following Joseph Brodsky

He is everywhere.
Russia, first and last and always
in between the smaller places:
London, New York, Hell,
even LA. But Norenskaia
and Palanga are larger,
the ground muddier,
the rain falling like a curtain
of iron, like cast iron buckets
that the women trudging home
carry, their old hair in scarves,
their calves, piano legs, in woolens,
unshaven, unseen, even when naked,
by their men, tired as plow horses,
vodka numb. Not sad, by God,
none sad even at Christmas.
Just another day. The star
they follow fits on a flag
and shines everywhere: the butcher shop,
the coal mine, the church now
a government office. You don't
have to be a wise man to see it,
but it would be unwise
not to notice.

Letter to Sister Mary Appassionata on Darkness and Light and David Citino

(for Pam)

Dear Sister,

I know you have given a lecture on light, where you touched, always with that alabaster hand with the joke buzzer hidden in your palm, upon the vagaries of vision: "There's nothing we can't see." So, I think you would appreciate this deep autumn morning with its gold confusion of leaves, its exodus of birds and the harvest of the blessed sugar beets. Fall, as you well know, is the season of winding down, the season of entropy and plain old chaos. But out of that comes this light, first introducing itself like a million pink flamingos rising as one above the eastern horizon. Was it you who said pink is the most dangerous color, so innocent and provocative at the same time? I've heard it is the universal color of tongues—yours, mine, Michael Jordan's airborne to a slam dunk, even that Hereford cow down the hill licking her newborn calf to life. Didn't one of the saints have his or her tongue cut out? I don't remember for what exactly, perhaps giving a mob of infidels the Bronx cheer.

Ah, I digress, though this light does the opposite. Now the flamingos have changed to brass, a million trumpets blaring the gospel of a new day. And yet, I hear a sadness in the light, a slight groan in the earth, a sigh in the trees, something about the nature of beginnings that always includes endings. I think it has something to do with this shadow or shade limning the perimeters of things like a dark halo, marking off each object in such a way that highlights its own contrast and unique individuality (so, so necessary in our ever-growing homogeneous world).

I believe this precious darkening is Providence's way of marking David's passing. Not away so much, as passing *into* this world, his words, images, thoughts, the very character of his being now dispersed part and parcel to encircle every particle and wave of light. So that no sunrise or sunset, no season no matter how cold, or how sweltering (Oh, those Ohio summers!) can be without this new shade of the holy. I think you said it best, "When we're patient with the dark it all takes shape and we become a part of heaven."

Bless you and David Citino,
A Former 8th Grader

An Unfinished Beer While Staring
at a Photograph of Faulkner

Caught off guard, without a drink,
outdoors, half-turned in his lawn chair,
the sub fusc lawn disappearing
into shadows behind him, perturbed,
older than he wants to be, but addicted
to the fame, the scowl a pose, no pen:
he's not working on anything in particular.

You could see me as younger,
purely anonymous, the beer a token—not
a gift so much as a souvenir
from the soundless fury of the past—when I grew
his moustache and practiced arrogance
I might have perfected if it hadn't been
for Bill's crack to his young daughter on her tenth birthday,
unwilling to leave his bourbon leisure
to join her party, "No one remembers
Shakespeare's daughter."

No light in August, but from my daughter's room:
"Daddy, read me a story." Not his child,
not this beer, not as I lay dying,
I run down the hall as if the barn
is burning.

Zen of Running

(following Gary Snyder)

On the whole

lycra pants neon blue
GRID "Shadow" shoe
                 with "sweet spot"

almost dawn, asphalt light
        past great telephone poles
        one after another, one
        at a time, a gauntlet
        of creosote, rough round wood

through the between, middle-less
middle of barley not yet born

nylon red jacket noisy
in the no wind

not just the tractored soil
ribbed flat but plantar fasciitis
"bone spurs" commonly "misnamed"
            (like buffalo, Indian Paintbrush, wapiti)

twinge the feet
a pain full reminder
where the earth is.

After "Burned"

(following Philip Levine)

Without looking where I was
going, stumbling over all
the broken glass, the rusting chrome,
in and out of the single-bulbed rooms,
the 40-watt blinking. I see only
two-dimensional playing cards
of women bent over brown sinks,
a cat black and gray in the corner,
through the sun-stained curtains
all the other windows with browned women
bent over scoured sinks. Jesus,
I'm nowhere and everywhere:
hills of skulls and barbershops
full of boys and men with the same crewcuts.

It's 1965, not clapboard or shotgun houses,
but powdery blue stucco, lime green fascia,
and daisy yellow goodness. Good Lord,
they called it Sun Ray Estates and
if it wasn't for the colors, we would have gone
home to a different house and not known
the difference. Except for my brother,
born a Jew (not chosen) in our Baptist congregation,
a negro (not African or American) in our Scotch-Irish clan,
you could tell by the way he skipped when we marched.

The ugly neighborhood snickered,
but only he read the beauty in mother's apron, in
her beehive hair-do, her bargain perfume and
cherry red nails he learned to polish.

Funny, I found no funerals or graves
despite all the elegies, all the limbs
underground, all the factories—
Detroit, Bergen-Belsen, Kolyma, Tule Lake—
colorless songs except for the finches,
small, feisty lighting up leaveless bushes
in Wyoming's winters when the day breaks
and stays unbroken until the last layer
of gray light goes dark and we know night
inside out, each of us a Jonah waiting
for some word within our Leviathan.
And while we wait we grow accustomed
to the whale silence, enough to dance
on the bottom of the belly, making bone music
with our knives and forks on the ribs,
not grave, not grave, no need to return
to the earth. It is there inside of us—
in these hands clapping in the dark,
sounds like a child crying or laughing;
it doesn't matter. Sounds like a child
echoing through the chambers, some iron,
some marble, some stucco loud as light:
ten thousand suns or single candle flame.

Despite all the unknowns, we only know
what to do from the gut, groping
for the child in the cooing darkness.

Following Rumi into the Wyoming Wind

How could anyone embrace this wind?
More howling than night.
Reach with your fingers for stars,
your heart a round gold moon,
and enfold the torrent to your breast.
Inhale now all the air of the world,
and exhaust yourself trying to run
to the end of time and back,
exhaling to the furthest corner of space.
See! Everywhere you go is the Beloved:
hear that in the wind, in your breathing.

Following Meister Eckhart and Rumi

These God drunk guys,
delirious with their escape from prisons
of dogma, dancing beneath
the towers, shouting at the guards,
giddy in the searchlight,
they juggle and dodge the bullets
oblivious to the warden's bullhorn
and the cheers of the prisoners.
They never quite run away.
God is sound, metaphor, language,
music. They know the sobering silence
of the cave is the death of God,
of theater. The grave, nothing more
than a hole in the ground:
no door, no ladder, shallow,
full of dirt that will quietly
blow away.

St. Francis and the Almond Tree

He opened his eyes in the dark room.
The candle, smallest light, danced
shadows on the bare walls and around
the crucifix that began to glow.
The wood was aflame, yet couldn't burn.
The figure bled light, the face, not in agony,
but eyes closed with the slightest smile.

Blinded by the vision, he stumbled out
into the bluecold dawn, his bare feet numb
on the stone path. Winter had emptied the garden,
shriveling vines, their browned and blackened stems
clean as the tiny skulls of flower heads.
The naked tree, more bone than bark, stood
glazed with ice, like death itself
contorted into a corpse in the frozen air.
His thin robe quivering, he stood

and murmured to the silent tree. *Tell me*
about God. Wordless, the limbs burst
into blossom, and he fell, his body curling
into a prayer of thanksgiving.
He peeked at the shining tree
and knew that belief was a thirst
and faith, water.

Dylan Thomas at Forty with Small Children

So just do it, like a Nike ad,
beginning with a number two pencil.
Then since it is five-thirty in the meadowlark
warbling yellow feathery sun-flowered morning,
a little black gurgle of coffee hot
and vapory strong but not primordial.
And maybe because your stomach has been
in a short drought having seen little vegetation
since last night's dinner was made
permanently incomplete by the baby's suffering
from gas, so wheeling in a good round
donut helps complete the circle
of preparations, being the perfectly
glazed limits around the infinite
space of the hole in the middle
of poetic possibilities where it is
only a gray matter of beginning,
and has nothing to do with tennis shoes.
So just do it.

Sex in High School

(after Neruda)

I have only lusted in my heart.
        –Jimmy Carter

I knew it was approaching taboo,
almost to the unhinging of trees,
of awakening nocturnal animals
in the middle of bright sun,
to let myself look, long and lingering, at the girl,
her breasts straining against the letter sweater
(an alphabet I'd never seen) following
the line of her back arched, a slim moon,
white as foam, hardly enough room for light
or my paralyzed hand, the fantasy of my palm
a starfish annealing to the salty skin
and then riding down the waves of her spine,
spreading out at the bottom
into mounds, melons, sculpted pink marble
and lost at last in the chasm winding to the underworld,
where Dante entered no doubt.

I fold my forty-year-old arms
in front of my chest, my hands
tucked under to hide the thought,
and I'm fine until I listen to the sky
and feel her eyes raining on me
the bluest rain flecked with too much sun,

so clear, I imagine pretending to fall in
but catch myself in the realization,
no matter how Mediterranean,
how crystalline the bay, I will be over
my head, that I never took the skin-diving lessons
required to explore this bed of coral and ivory
and smooth silvery stones polished into mirrors
that reflect emerald seas
eddying in the vermillion of youth.
It's a place I've never been,
never heard about, never believed existed,
but died to be there, or at least dreamed
the origin of earth that needs no land or wind
to be its own ground, to sing its own air.

To the Lighthouse
(for Virginia Woolf)

O Virginia, you beautiful neurotic,
if only I'd met you before you gathered the stones
as ye may, filling your pockets like lead posies,
until heavier than the weight of the world
you could not bear, and returned you to the earth
through a door in the river that closed behind you—
the seamless jambs, the liquid lock,
the antediluvian truth: you can never
step in the same river twice.

I would have had time to sew
the greatest coat, a hundred threads stronger
and a thousand hues brighter than Joseph's,
and as Raleigh laid it ever so gently over the water.
So, not even your constant shadow
would have gotten wet.

I know you were clever,
carefully picking up the rocks.
Cleverly, I would have pretended to help:
"Not that little piece of limestone,
look at this—quartz laced rock,
heavy as a meteorite, its weight perfect,
so earth bound, so useless for skipping
across the beaming surface. See—

shiny speckles like silver or sterling faces
of a thousand tiny pocket watches—
time is such a fluid thing."

Oh, Heraclitus had that right,
but only the number, not the beauty of it.
He was hung up on banks, channels,
logjams, oxbows, pools—you know
it's not the course but the waves,
patternless, undulating stars, that matter.

O I forgot dear, the stones remind
you of the bombs falling on London.
But try to see the smaller picture for once—
this stone here, onyx, obsidian,
black enough to be exotic,
shiny as the dark side of the moon,
unlit forever. They say (those
old Antiquarians you complained about)
that this one is the same as the sculpted flesh
of the black Madonna, that holy relic (they claim)
that survived all those bombs dropped on Poland.
No, it's not sacred or magical, believe me,
it's nothing really, like a mark on a wall,
so dark, so small you need a lighthouse to see,
though you know only a single candle flame
brings a moth to the light. Please, here,
save it for a few moments of being.

Fourth of July, Powell, Wyoming

(following Jim Harrison)

Not late by summer standards,
but too long after midnight,
drinking beer, dark Mexican hops,
God knows what the Aztecs would think,
this watered down Mayan brew sold
for eight bucks a six pack and drunk
by new conquistadors at barbecues
watching fourth of July fireworks
over backyard fences, their dogs hiding
under redwood decks.

Not tonight, not twelve miles from town,
wearing my own feathered headdress,
I'm the only one awake
except for a widowed farm wife's peacock
a couple of farms away, an anathema
(the peacock not the widow)
for the surviving farmers: its falsetto arias
have nothing to do with bombs bursting in air,
fanning its tail like a flag of neither power nor glory,
but only in waves, amber (as well as
blue and green) for a hen's love
in the dawn's early light.

Following Cold Mountain (Han-Shan)

Comparisons are odious.
            —Nietzsche

I'm no hermit like Cold Mountain:
daughters and dogs, a constant wife
and some cats constantly
orbiting about me on this bluff
a dozen miles from town
down a dirt road in the dark lap
of Heart Mountain.
I'm no monk like Han-Shan,
here prayer is wind,
cold, constant, fierce:
where faith is an anvil
for a wind chime
and God is sagebrush,
ubiquitous graygreen, aromatic
and impervious to the unbeliever.

Postcard to William Stafford

O Bill, you're right.
Something, even a seed,
a piece of lint—no matter—
a word is enough, of course,
to build a nest. The twigs,
the leaves will come,
and eventually after ten
thousand days, even
just before midnight like this,
so tired, I can hardly stand up:
an oak, a poem.

After Reading Rilke's Biography
Listening to Debussy

(Prelude to the Afternoon of a Faun)

It took nine months to come
to this, after five hundred pages,
I read your life slowly, like an old lover
allowed to visit one last time.

Maybe because it's all wind tonight,
riffling layers of it, wild without remorse,
so that helpless, shrunken, we crawl
either to our beds or your poetry.
And there embrace what we do not understand.

Surely you, in Muzot, in your slim flesh danced,
no Nijinsky, those first fawn-like steps,
the sound of polished marble, of rarefied solitude
caught by the sinewy clarinet.

That's it, of course, poetry—it's all you were,
or *what* you were—despite the petty human gnawing
at your knuckles sitting amongst the squalor
of your relationships. You didn't walk
but curved inward, becoming parabola,
and outward in widening gyres—
you name it, but you were pure circulation,
the movement of angels.

I lean back into this weltering dark
made poignant by the moths
mashed against the screen—to hell with the black
avalanche of air, the moonlessness of it all—
it's this small light, forty-watt bulb, naked, lampless
that is to be caressed (to death if necessary)
to behold, and beholden to.

Sometimes a Raven

(after Poe)

Sometimes I'm Edgar,
dressed in a black cloak,
top hat, cane, macabre,
taking myself or my night
mares too seriously.

Wherever I walk, there's a fog,
night, docks, shadows
of women smoking in doorways.

I'm not surprised by the gas
street lamps or a horse and buggy
clopping across a cobblestone street.

I hear patent leather footsteps
behind me. There are no policemen,
only alleys, garbage cans, and cats
black as ravens.

It's difficult to imagine
my day life, the kids, wife, bills,
my dull job in a fluorescent office,
and bills, hells bells! bills.

I feel torn between
a golf game on Sunday

and a dark café on the Rue Morgue
with a glass of absinthe.

Either way, I'd be dead
or completely mad
without poetry.

After Work

(after William Carlos Williams)

The work day still panting
after me, I reach for an idea
out of nowhere—nearly numb
in a recliner by the window
reddening with sunset—and grab some
thing, slippery with muddled thoughts.

I feel for a few words, all ill-fitting,
but enough for this to depend upon
despite the broken wheel barrow,
the dead white chickens,
and the glazed absence of rain water.

Reading Cold Mountain's Poetry, Listening to Fauré's Requiem

Where there's death, there's beauty.
May Day ends as it began—utterly clear,
a transparent riddle: everyone can solve it,
except the man who saw both sides of the sun.

For him, there's only this strangely familiar,
green mystery, these pink and yellow explosions
in the garden. And yet, almost, this blue
black sky makes sense—the bruised logic of night
erasing shapes of leaves until a half round moon
throws its absurd light everywhere.

And he forgets where he is finally,
and stays lost as long as he can.
Like Yang Hsiu, the moment he sees
a young woman, *Kyrie Eleison,*
he knows mystery.

After Reading Cavafy in
Barnes & Noble, Billings, MT

I know he's Greek, God
dammit. Since day one
his tribe used only the human scale
to weight the world. You know: Zeus, Apollo,
Aphrodite, cattle lovely Io.
No matter what: the bearded lightning,
the goldilocked sun, spring, a runaway girl,
and a bevy of flora that used to preen,
run, jump, and gossip: narcissus, the laurel,
echo—that girl who loved Love
and ended up getting wings
and a snout filled with pollen.

Even the night skies were filled
with diamond studded muscles
and breasts. So, who can blame him,
if his lean imagery is covered by downy skin,
perfumed hair, ripe olive lips, as he gazed across centuries
or an Alexandrian street, always finding
somebody who lost his kingdom,
or his farm or his love, and always his life,
adding to Homer's innumerable shades.

But I lust for the glinting sand,
the brutal light, and all those aquamarine bodies
of water, even the bony temples

of fractured marble and contusions of stone.
And if it has got to be somebody,
please, once, my dear Cavafy, let loose
some of those wild haired women,
brazen spangling widows and young mothers.
Surely Aphrodite wasn't a whore: thrust
into some god awful arranged marriage
to a gimpy, workaholic with dirty hands.

But I'm here, far north, a bookstore café,
an afterthought, a good afterthought, drinking
too much dark coffee drowning in too many damn books,
too many damn good books, after I've done the good hubby-
daddy duty hunting like an anemic Orion
for plastic bowls and laundry soap at Costco
(a Trojan horse warehouse stuffed with too much damn stuff
not damn good stuff).

Feeling torn to pieces, *sparagmos,*
by consumer America's Dionysian cult (ure).
I've escaped with you old gay Greek poet,
who's breathless, spare, nonflammable,
direct as a newspaper with a little gossip,
a little diary at times, and some honest
to goodness lust too. Who has
goaded me into an odyssey
of observing a current myth.

The table next to mine, a dead
ringer for a college professor,

middle-aged, ear-ringed,
with a note pad, sits sipping
his cappuccino, ridiculously aloof
in his bookish air. He seems
to be waiting with a hint
of expectation. He's not sure
what to do with the notepad,
writing not really his forte.

In she walks, single, divorced mom
with two kids (boys, I hear in her
exasperated narrative), cradling a couple
of poems a teacher liked a decade ago,
when she was cute. The jean shorts are the link
to that semester when they exacted a promise
from a blonde-bearded teacher to look
them over.

He offers to buy her a drink,
a Frappuccino, fruity coffee coed drink.
She allows this move, in fact
she's planned it. After all,
she's brought a notebook—some "silly things"
she managed to jot down after the boys
were in bed (after their father left unable
to offer anything after his letter sweater).

The window promises little light left,
August fading and still no gold leaves on the horizon;
only a cave blue future of forced hibernation

they both fear and desire. Oh, I'm afraid,
my dear Cavafy, no Greek tragedy here,
only a couple of would-be actors
unable to fake real tears.

A Long Way from Amherst
(following Emily Dickinson)

I'm here after midnight,
all alone. It is not the time,
or the space, daughter crowded
and a twenty-yeared wife.

Surrounded by the living
room—there is nothing
wrong, you know,
with this all alone.

I asked for it,
praying to no one
in particular, and was answered.
All my life without question
it has been where I have been
saved or reborn again and again.

Even with night like this,
blacker than any ideas
of sunless hours, unlit
where brightness has never been,
a darkest darkness, leaving me
an island, all sand
save for a single palm,
a cliché *sans* Crusoe—

Yes, but gloriously Here,
though almost erased
to the point of pointlessness,
sitting in the pure poetry
of this Being all alone.

Russia's Lost Treasure

(for Anna Akhmatova)

It's too cold for April,
even for Wyoming,
or St. Petersburg.
The ponds have melted
and re-iced over, freezing
hope again everywhere,
even deserts of death
and dying. You know
the feeling of promises
reneged, of unrequited everything.

Tonight, I think of you,
so far away lying in your grave
country, your life long
ache. Those dead husbands
who didn't deserve death
despite their failing
to grasp the quicksilver
in you. Your wintry heart,
bloody snow. The ice no
more than grist for your mill,
like the Bolsheviks or that dark
fallen man Stalin. You lived

and outlived them all. Your inner
life made precious by exposure

to the outer cruelties of the world.
You, a radium isotope above ground
(and below), poetry a toxin
in the toxic veins, glowing, hot
figure of female earth shaped
by everything but the State,
shaped by Mother Russia
who holds you still
to her troubled breast,
holds you, hope, buried to be found
again, the treasure treasured.

Bloomsday, Wyoming

(following James Joyce)

Damn near Dublin weather today:
a mash of lumpy clouds stuck
on the bottom of a stainless-steel sky.
We're wrestling with the great expectations
of late spring that *sumer is icumen in.*
Here a thousand miles from the sea,
for Christ's sake, this salt taste
is only alkali, these swells and chicane—
wind gusting with nowhere to go,
these dolphins, dogs chasing balls,
that humpback whale, a cow in labor,
and the *Seirēnes* are just sirens
singing to no one except horseless
cowboys taking their last ride.

I sink my shovel in the garden
still not seeded, an empty pole,
hookless, baitless, and I think
of you, Joyce, hunched over
your table, half blind,
your glasses like goggles
as you dove deep, holding
your breath until the language burst,
rhetorical bubbles rushing to the surface
and still you didn't drown, but grew
gills and scales that glistened like mirrors

in which a landlubber like me could catch
his reflection if he tried.

I tried until I was blue in the face,
swimming with only a scarf
to keep me afloat, toward the dry
land, the driest land, the drought
in its fifth year, where my daughter,
like Nausicaä, grinning, needing no words
to save me, saved me with her paper
winnowing fan.

Faust in the Garden
(after Gounod after Goethe)

Isn't this it, where man opens
himself, inside out, to the scent
of Other. Not just the flowering
skin of the girl, pastel smooth
and ambered with sable arms,
not the honeyed calves, the thighs
dipped in cream with a molasses
desire there where the dream
of other dreams are to be felt,
beyond the time of words,
the compulsion to say what it is.
Isn't it when there is no need
for saying anything that we think
is the devil's way. So we substitute
our pure impulses for declarations
of affection, recitatives of naked apes.
Our monkey ancestors laugh at us,
hanging from thick trees, fruitless,
clattering for substance, for some
belief, man, in the girl's bird sighs,
or to have some faith at least
in our chartreuse passion
in the heavy moonless air.

Love Song of a Homeowner
(following John Updike)

Why is it you always feel as if you should be somewhere
else? Not just outside these pale walls, out from under
this sun wounded roof (shingles like scabs that won't heal),
past the closet of button-down shirts, pressed blue mirrors of each other,
the khaki, loose pants, "tan always in style,"
the wife comments from behind the bathroom door,
whispers of blush brushed on, clink of tweezers on the sink.

It's the omniscient narrator that sticks in your head
as you drift outside where it is genuinely bright
and the sunglasses are god knows where,
so, you squint to the car, but have forgotten the keys,
and rather than go back to retrieve them
(the sound of water and tooth brushing),
you continue walking down the driveway
past the sprinkler (it should be moved)
and unconsciously further away from the property
than you've been since you bought the place.

Only twice before, when the terrier was missing
and mistakenly you thought the neighbors might know.
The other time—when was that? That only once
summer night stroll, the two of you,
when she was eight months along
and couldn't go far. And now, past that,
heading around the corner, turning away from the main avenue,

the route to work and groceries and videos on Saturdays,
but left and then left again toward the sewage
treatment plant on the edge of town, lit like a constellation.

You don't linger, but cross, instead, the road
to where fields are, old farmland corn, alfalfa—hard-to-say—
broken glass for a while, crumpled cigarette packs,
bleached out in the moonlight (it's that late already),
but bright enough to find your way.
There's a breeze with the smell of woods
that stand at the edge of the river, its scree,
roadless banks, not even fishermen come here,
but that's where you enter the water.

It clings to your pants like Saran wrap,
but not too deep, knee high, a slow wade
to an ancient skiff tied to the cattails, an oar
inside, you half-climb, half roll in, lean over
the side, grabbing the rope, and pull to the knotted
end. Untying it, you let the boat drift
on its own, let the river take it slow,
without obstacles. The sky overhead riddled
with stars, you guess at a few until there are none you recognize,
but it doesn't matter as you lie down on the bottom
and dream of wind that will blow you to kingdom come
or down the river to where it dumps into the sea.

You'll row then, like Odysseus, cursing ancient gods
to get their attention, to hurl lightning at you,
to wreck on some unknown island, to be found

by some nymph, who will bathe your salted bones,
offering you wine, and, if not eternal life, then to die
in her gold braceleted arms, mortgage free.

Every Day I Write (in Time of War)

(after Robert Lowell)

I hear him, not every day,
make this declaration,
causing me to wince.
His mask fleshes smooth,
eyeless as Comus, a grin,
lightning without the fear of thunder.
Terrence, this is stupid stuff, indeed.

So where are his poems?
I have his journal here, the pages like mirrors
mirroring mirrors ad infinitum.
But after so many reflections of reflections,
it is impossible to find the Prime Mover,
and nothing found at last.

What of this real stuff—call it world,
it doesn't matter, blurry, unfixed, yet
still the same old rhetoric pinned
like lines of medals onto blue serge power
suits, blood red ties smeared down marble
white shirts, puffed out with air
more weighted than words.

There's a face bobbing there, too,
right up against the television screen,
surrounded by bubbles, benign as a turtle,

except for the sound of a dorsal fin
cutting the surface. Even the half-deaf fool,
listening to his own fictitious roar,
hunched over his desk, hears it,

but is too preoccupied with the motes
inside a certain slant of light. He's trying
to make a pattern out of their random purity.
Getting it wrong on purpose so he can see
better. Not sun or moon, but the bright dust
stirred up like a recurring nightmare
of a battlefield filling up with bodies
like grains of sand.

Why No One Writes Like Thomas Wolfe

You can't do it, not anymore. Not just not go
home. The million-footed creature
of those magnificent steel and glass
and newly cemented cities does not exist
anymore. We are not that generic,
the "types": ethnic and class don't exist,
never did except by distance and lack
of familiarity. No Jews, no Okies, no
Japs, no inscrutable Chinese shuffling by
in pigtails on their way to the laundry
in slippers, brocaded jackets, and pajamas.
No tycoons, big bellied vests with solid gold
pocket watches and silver chains, no time
told through great walrus mustaches.
And no locomotives chugging steam, no hoboing,
no Jimmy Rogers train songs yodeling.
No paddy-wagoned, billy-clubbed flat foots,
whiskey red jowled and brogued tongues.
No monstrous wild writers shut up
in their cold-water flats writing monstrous tomes on top
of Sylvania refrigerators. None of that.

We've got nice, accredited creative
writing programs now, where you learn
all about hooks and pithy topic-sentenced
short paragraphs, suddenly bereft of adverbs,
and for God's sake keep it succinct. Remember

the real work lies in the pitch, the query
letter, the marketing strategy.

Oh, to catch that last ferry with you Tom, top deck,
the spray of Canadian waters, in a Mackinaw,
to refuse the drunk's bottle,
even slap it out of the tubercular hand,
knocking it into the Prince William Sound,
watching it sink. We laugh and head
for a bar and a room with a blinking neon sign
outside the window. No air conditioning,
steam heated room, a hotel keep, who looks
a little like Valentino, grins knowing a gal
named Marlene or Jean is lying across your bed
with sun-coiled hair in a satin gown that clings
like second skin. She asks for a light, and
through the curling smoke, she smiles and subtle
as black and white can be, coos,
You're an angel. Welcome home.

Lament for a Wyoming Poet Laureate
(for Charles Levendosky)

Not much alike, I thought, at first:
me and this round bearded, wild
haired poet with Jerry Garcia
glasses that magnified dark
dancing eyes. Merry and

mad at all the things I was
starting to awaken to.
I liked his merriment
and was nervous about his intensity.
His politics, I glibly tossed off.
I couldn't fathom.
Unfathomable he agreed—
that's the problem.

Later his generosity preceded
him and lingered after he left,
taking the time to take
one of my poems and thanking me!
before I thought to thank him.

Ah, Charles, I regret
not getting closer, though we
laughed at our mutual idiocy,
writing a poem while driving,

both of us ending
in a ditch. Worth it: not
the poem, but the compulsion
and its retelling.

His passion, his courage,
witnessing the execution;
blood on everything:
victims, criminals, and the
righteous apathetic. The moon
glowed red that night.

He wasn't one for abstractions.
I heard about the cancer,
the imminent death. How
chemo left him hairless, so
he had a new photo printed
for his column and left
death waiting. Tom said
you were making a comeback,
writing again, an award, two.
Then I didn't hear
anything until tonight
except whispers about
hospice at home.

You'd like this, Charles,
on the night you died, the last
of winter was still growling outside,

more silhouette than substance,
but a real wind,
loud and right against
the little conservative houses.

Winter in Byron's Wake

I can almost hear the minute flakes of snow falling
like notes of a Chopin etude,
almost inconsequential, almost
invisible. They barely know how to fall,
but swirl, willy-nilly, lightly
touching the ground, snow sprites dancing
a moment, the earth whitening
beneath their feet, a pirouette of wind
and gone: the world none the worse
for the wear.

Only in winter, deep—after
the colorful shock of Fall,
do the trees achieve intricacy,
mosaics, hieroglyphics, brandings,
their mandalas of limbs relieved
of the clotted green. Uncluttered at last
of all those fluttering leaves, they sing
bold, rude, their nude limbs ravished
by the rough palms of wind,
the kneading snow, massaged
by icy air and cold caresses
from an aloof sun, yellow in the leaf.

At the Reading of the Wyoming Poet Laureate
(for Robert Roripaugh)

I imagined from his picture
the bald man mumbling in the pit
of the library in that stodgy Victorian manner,
half expecting to see him in sepia tones,
high collared, side-whiskered, old
fashioned scowl.

But that was just a first impression,
the shallowest of eyesight,
a speck of dust would blind it.
So, squinting, I looked again, further,
trying on telescopes, a long silver glass look,
a stellar look. And I saw follicles of light
where his hair used to be.

Within that skinned brightness,
words began to lope and then gallop
sand colored words, gully shaped,
making drought noises that blew
into full-blown stories about all the round pegs
in this square state: Indian women,
Mormon girls, Japanese wives, deer
during hunting season, and traps
full of God's children.

Until listening so closely,
I couldn't see anymore,
and knowing full well
that if he went half a league onward,
I would end up an anachronism
of tears and laughter.

After the Fall

(In Remembrance of 9/11)

I stayed up late reading *Ecclesiastes*
as if I had never read it before.
Vanity of vanities. Indeed.
The wise man will suffer
the same fate as the fool.
I look out at the dim moon,
not enough light to make a difference.

On this bitter end of November,
seven degrees above zero,
Autumn done with dying.
Most creatures gone or hiding,
drawn into death or their own
sense of ground.

I watch a cottonwood's withdrawal,
its willingness to let go: leaves
and color, shade, shelter,
losing its desire for liquid, light,
and the luxury of heat.

Among the limbs, the migration from nests,
their rough grace of ten thousand interlacings,
once filled with the small, loud hungers
that grew into flights, *feeding on the wind,*
when the fateful emptying began:

one after another, always,
to the inescapable south.

Winter is not the only risk of growth—
fire, infestation, chain saw—
but circumventing that to go skeletal:
to sap shrunken, hardening inside
a frozen trunk, its bark girdled by snow,
its branches already skinned
and boned beneath iron clouds.

As this steel wind, bitter and bladed
slices through the forest, sounding
a cold history of carvings, fellings, hangings….
Maybe some things change. Still
suns come and go, like bombs and lightning,
treehouses and swings, tires on a rope.

I cannot suffer anyone's fate,
but my own, obscure or luminous,
like Keats' epitaph: here lies us all
whose lives are writ on water.
Means are all I can grasp, not ends:
the ludicrous grace in writing a poem.

Is this any way to right the Towers again—
once rectangled giants of steel sinew
and muscular glass, nothing in themselves—

now resurrected, *creatio ex nihilo*, into
a purer symbol? To everything turn, turn,

I turn to my love, asleep on the far side
of the bed, though within my reach,
the sound of her breath, a sigh, a soft moan,
an invitation to her dream. Holy of Holies!
All is not vanity.

Falling
(after Keats)

Autumn can't be drawn by broad strokes,
no wide, horse-haired brush,
stallion tail slapping the air.
So, still this twilight, it settles
inside small envelopes,
lacquered, gilded, used before,
sealed and unsealed with a whiff
of some primeval perfume,
vermillion scented, a hint of plum
dissipating into the deep red end
of things turning purple, indigo,
these last swaths of color on the horizon.

All so layered you'd think this is all
there is to it—but hardly that simple
or that silent: the sound of cocoons closing
and stones, small round, slate colored things,
rumbling along the creek bed.
This autumn day ends wrapping her foliage
around the still air, an invisible child,
whose breath is edged with frost.

So, we practice silence to listen
to the sap beating in the pine,
the heart of the world just hidden

on the dark banks, under a new moon,
black and empty before waxing in an unlit sky.
No seams to any of it, no lines to cross,
nothing to decipher—like autumn itself,
falling into a full absence.

An Open Apology to Robert Haas
on the 25th Anniversary of Janis Joplin's Death

I'm sorry Bob that I threw you over
for long dead Janis
doing "Ball and Chain" at Woodstock.
I was eighteen that summer,
just out of high school,
just out in the world working
forty-two days straight,
twelve to seventeen hours a day
(overtime only after fifty hours a week)
in a cold storage plant
during pear season.

I worked on my poetry,
driving a forklift in and out
of refrigerated warehouses,
kept at forty degrees Fahrenheit.
I wore two coats, gloves, ski hat,
boots, wool socks, and still froze,
sitting in the 100-degree sun at noon
(Sacramento in July) only taking off
one of the coats.

On the forty-second day, I snapped.
Someone had broken a crate of pears
and left it in one of the warehouses.
I was blamed by a foreman
who relished belittling the workers.
I chased him down two flights

of stairs and across the parking lot
to the manager's office where he
locked himself inside, yelling out
I was fired to my yelling in,
I quit.

The forty-nine Pontiac I drove
the twenty miles of river road
home didn't have a radio.
I never heard Janis or about Woodstock
until I saw it on the evening news,
watching old, wonderful Walter Cronkite
reporting with a bemused smile,
as I ate a TV dinner (*Swanson*) on a pear crate.

So, when the blues hour came on tonight,
the same time you, Bob, were reading
poetry on National Public Radio,
I turned the dial and wept,
like a blues harmonica, listening
to that throaty moan of Janis Joplin's
crazed, whiskyed love of life pouring out
until it overflowed, like the tears
of your "immense, illiterate,
consoling angels."

The Beat Season
(after Jack Kerouac)

In the grace and beauty of the dying season,
the wind glasses into light in clear rectangular sheets,
while the light brilliances back into wind,
of serrated ocher, the stuff of lost leaves
losing their sense of limbs, disembarked and sap free—
a woodless vision that torments ex-lumberjacks and ex-squirrels.
But we, who stumbled over the calendar's phrase,
"Autumnal Equinox," shrug and enter,
virtually happy, our chat rooms.
While what's left of nature (an anonymous martyrdom),
with its patient lack of expectations, despite winter
being a smooth, round stone's throw away,
shrugs too.

On Antelopes and Beats in Wyoming

They used to have to go fast,
thoughtless as an empty headed buddha,
but not careless, never careless,
just fast and hard. For burroughs
and jack it was nothing
but edges (the Angle Bar),
corners, and everything concrete
and so vertical the sky not high enough.
Thank God for that round road.

I dig it here where it's easy being beat,
but not fast, not mindless, but no mind,
antelope mind, all that speed perfectly still
in the middle of the pure horizontal,
as far as an elephantine eye can see,
forever at least and careful.

In the alfalfa now of summer
blooms the bone lotus of winter,
so, we never go light, always a pair
of long-johns in the pickup—polypropylene
like the hairs on the antelope's flanks:
tubal and erect in July to catch a breeze,
or December laying it down, double layering
when icicles hang like crystal crucifixes,
so cool in the dead blue air.

Aeneas & Dido After Reading Dugan

Yeah, that's always the way
isn't it? The hero after sex
slips out of bed, grabs his sandals,
wallet, and spear (tiptoeing
to the door) red from the exertion.

He can't look at the royal body,
all that resignation and offering, that chalice
too sacred, that cup too heady, that drink
from where he fell head over heels drunk
without a drop.

With duty stamped on his firm upper lip,
he announces his allegiance to something
higher and stops. Looking at his chief advisor,
he asks, "What's that word for duty?"
"Ecumenical, Prince." "Ah, yes,
it's my...duty!" his finger pointing
at the empty sky.

There was nothing higher, she knew,
colder perhaps, more abstract and false,
the way of the world dear, he bluffed.
She flung back the sheets. "The joke
is on you, Prince. You lost one war,
and leaving, you lose another."

An Open Letter to Jacques Prévert

How? Is it possible? That after all this time (no need to count)
I have encountered you only now? Through this remnant
of your long dead life: in two books—referenced and quoted,
your poem, "How to paint a bird!" explained by two others,
a not dead poet and a never dead Zen master. And you
there in a photograph atop the literary calendar for the month of July,
your short-buzzed hair, your so very French black t-shirt,
the stub of a cigarette stuck in your mouth as you lean over
your café table. A carafe of chardonnay at your elbow,
your puffy eyes dark in concentration on cutting
an apple, the same as writing a poem, crisp, red skin
begin anywhere: above, side, middle—*in media res*—
with something sharp, slice or carve, peel, puncture
or whittle. The point is to get below the surface,
to reveal the pulp, the flesh, the seeds there all the time
to grow, release the aroma of soul, pure, unblemished,
to taste. Ah! the essence of poems and apples—fresh,
sweet, juice of life. The checkered cloth napkin on your lap
catching pieces of fruit and light and shadow. After all
this time, you've been waiting to offer me a bite.

Merci,
B.

A Hint of Rimbaud in Wyoming

Autumn slithered loudly,
cold-blooded with a steel breath
ringing the trees in the black-hooded
night. The air smelled of serpent's laughter:
slow, fat, swallowing its own tail
in a dream of cactus flowers.

Listening to Górecki's Third Symphony as a Light Snow Falls

Begins beyond the porcelain mountains
on the other side of where the sky was
without a sound at first, yet with a sense
of something on its way.

Beneath this layer of cold swan feathers,
a ground beats like a great bell,
reverberating so slowly, overlapping,
merging into one seamless ringing,
and so close to silence that only the bones know
enough to look up at the piccolo flakes

piping through the air, little girls
in pinafores, their slips showing
as they skip and cartwheel,
giggling as they fall oblivious
of the groaning earth which they tease,

mischievously grabbing at its old limbs,
leafless, arthritic, having not danced
forever, not this way, naked,
wildly atop the great frozen corpse
of the world, they thumb their little white noses
at the old hoary absence of things.

Their play turns serious,
though not dark, not even somber,
just pensive, referential, hymnal,

the notes falling in choirs,
in harmonious refrains—no solos,
soprano or alto—they sing praises
to sacred motion and change,
each a tiny light, a heatless particle
of luminous presence. The sky,
once aloof, blue-blooded, now
descends, bowing to the purified earth,
clothed, hooded, veiled, virginal
again, shimmering with expectation
at this annunciation.

Blizzard

(following Katagiri Roshi)

Winter is a constant manifestation of beauty itself.
                    —Dainin Katagiri

Strung out like shredded sheets, this snow
unnerves things, a whitened wind
at full strength: seen! at last.
A swarm of sugared bees
or bleached starlings bending
folding, unraveling—there is no
containment but this whirling balloon,
waxing and waning like some gaseous moon.
Even with squinting eyes
and grimacing face, with numbed hands
and frozen feet I feel this constant
manifestation of beauty itself.
Cold to the core, purified and flung like chaff:
where, there, here, everywhere,
snow.

Silver Gate, Montana

(following Richard Hugo)

After the rain fell like silver
bullets, I watched buffalo
ford Soda Butte Creek
and cross the road to the chagrin
of a red Hummer
that damn near knocked
an old bull squirrelly—though
I'd like to have seen the damage
done to that monstrosity (the SUV
not the bison). But the rain drove
us all away at twilight: the bull
up the hill into one last crowd
of cows, the red Hummer, I hope,
to the third or fourth circle of hell,
and me to here where I don't think
Dick ever stopped.

The name would have grabbed him,
I'm sure, but no bars to speak of—
four miles further, Cooke City
would have been his spot.
Not here where I've landed in August
when this place is a runoff for tourists
spilling into Yellowstone.
The mountains almost swallow
this townless town—it's salvation.
You stop here, and like Moses
in the middle of the parted Red Sea,

you sense you'll make it.
Because mountains are the tangible
miracles of the world, where the tides
of the far-reaching oceans can't reach.

Locals here know, Moose and Bear first,
these peaks are the source of rivers,
the repository of winter snow.
Here the world rises above its grand
pettiness. Armies (forget Hannibal)
don't make it. Walmart, too, meets
its match. Corporate America
can't figure out what to do
with such incline and girth,
such resolution and patience.
The gods didn't live on Olympus.
They were Olympus. We need
no mythologies. Mountains are.

Listening to Maya Angelou

Molasses in a coffee voice,
sweet black with real cream.
There's heat just simmering, no boil.

Something outside the kitchen, too
moist, humid rich soil
and trees, Lord, trees—
hardwood, teak, mahogany,

but able to bend, for the roots are deep,
supple, like the wise fingers of old women
kneading dough.

Following Mary Oliver

Tomorrow I will go to the woods,
not today, and see the forest
for the trees. Here lodgepole
pine, there subalpine fir,
a quivering stand of aspen.
Further where there is no forest,
only crooked gullies
trickling spring melt, I'll
find a cottonwood, least
heralded, alone, and embrace
its corrugated bark,
and climb up into its gnarled
crown, and listen to the
silver leaves raspy wisdom
about weather and age.

Open Letter to Rabindranath Tagore

Forgive me, great man, Mahatma,
unlike you, I can appeal to no master,
to either bow to his feet
or dance whirling until I drop
in ecstasy, in pure adoration.

Flowers I pluck will droop
of their nature and I'll have no garland
to offer for any lover. Neither
can I appeal to any Father,
cloud glorious and all knowing.

My sire, flesh, blood, and bones
to dust, only lived with his feet
on the ground. Nor can I pledge
to any Son, emaciated, hungry too
for a father and master, willing
to do all for such hopes and dreams.
Not to Him either can I appeal,
despite his bright rags, his thorned brow,
and nailed passion.

I'll look, instead, with eyes closed, inside
for nothing—no image, no master to behold—
but to see, to sense that it is in the appeal,
the effort that any master exists:

faceless, fatherless, a breath, a pulse,
and know the world is divine
in its ephemeral appearance. This,
great poet, is the reedless reed
through which I sing.

In the Footprints of Whitman

There's no following Walt, at least not close catching him
by the coat tails as it were. He's far ahead, even a hundred years
behind because he walks no straight path, but is a path himself,
circumnavigating time and space, you and me.

I catch sight of him only in his circling just within and beyond my own
orbit.
Look! there: a body of molten light, there: a body of glacial fire,
now, of liquid wind, ah! yes, and a body of ten thousand blades
of eternally growing grass.

I see him and kick off my shoes to walk barefoot,
my naked nerve endings across his celebrated earth.
O it's dirt alright, and because of its grit and debris and chert,
I can, at least, feel my way after him.

Should I lie down there where the grass has been imprinted
by the loafing and inviting of his soul?
My barbaric shout: Yes!
Spreading my arms wide, my legs swinging open and closed like a child
making green snow angels on a summer lawn.

It just takes a little imagination, a little lack of self-consciousness
about what others may say. Instead, all you need is a little effort
to embrace the cosmos of Me and the universe of Not-Me.

Do I contradict myself?
I am large too, containing multitudes, and contained
by Walt as well. Verily I cannot contradict myself.

Look here, you, too, see the path ever there
winding wherever. Follow it. It's not about catching up with me or him,
it's just about following.

About the Author

Burt Bradley lives on a bluff in Northwest Wyoming seventy miles from Yellowstone National Park. For over thirty years, with his wife Janet, a photographer, he has delved into the wild serenity of the greater Yellowstone ecosystem. His writing has appeared in *Ring of Fire: Writers of the Yellowstone Region, Michigan Quarterly Review, Best of Writers at Work*, among others. He is currently professor emeritus at Northwest College in Powell, Wyoming, where he taught Writing in the Wild classes in Yellowstone and the Southwest Desert.

WAYFARER

BASED IN THE PIONEER VALLEY, MASS.

At Wayfarer Books we believe poetry is the language of the earth. We believe words—shaped like rivers through wild places—can change the shape of the world. We publish poets and writers and renegades who stand outside of mainstream culture—poets, essayists, and storytellers whose work might withstand the scrutiny of crows and coyotes, those who are cryptic and floral, the crepuscular, and the queer-at-heart. We are more than just a publisher but a community of writers. Our mission is to produce books that can serve as a compass and map to all wayfarers through wild terrain.

wayfarerbooks.org